THE ARCHITECTURE OF ANIMALS

THE EQUINOX GUIDE TO WILDLIFE STRUCTURES

ADRIAN FORSYTH

CAMDEN HOUSE

© Copyright 1989 by Camden House
Publishing (a division of Telemedia
Publishing Inc.)

All rights reserved. The use of any
part of this publication, reproduced,
transmitted in any form or by any means,
electronic, mechanical, photocopying,
recording or otherwise, or stored in a
retrieval system, without the prior consent
of the Publisher, is an infringement of the
copyright law and is forbidden.

Canadian Cataloguing in Publication Data

Forsyth, Adrian
  The architecture of animals

Includes index.
ISBN 0-920656-16-1 (bound)
ISBN 0-920656-08-0 (pbk.)

1. Animals – Habitations –Juvenile literature.
I. Title.

QL756.F67   1989   j591.56′4   C89-093836-9

Front Cover: Rod Planck, Tom Stack & Associates

Back Cover: Wayne Lynch

Trade distribution by: Firefly Books
250 Sparks Avenue
Willowdale, Ontario M2H 2S4

Printed in Canada for:
Camden House Publishing
7 Queen Victoria Road
Camden East, Ontario K0K 1J0

Designed by: Ulrike Bender

Editor: Laurel Aziz

Colour separations by: Colour Technologies
Toronto, Ontario

Printed and bound in Canada by:
D.W. Friesen & Sons Ltd.
Altona, Manitoba

Printed on 70 lb. Friesen Matte

C O N T E N T S

The snapping turtle is the largest freshwater turtle in Canada, measuring almost 20 inches in length and weighing up to 50 pounds. Although the snapper is an aquatic species that inhabits streams, marshes and lakes, it crawls onto land to lay its white and pink eggs in a nest it digs in the sand. Sometimes, snapping turtles deposit their eggs in the vegetation of a muskrat lodge. Although this location is efficient for incubating the eggs, it is not secure, since the muskrat feeds on both the eggs and the young turtles.

One day, I watched a squirrel scrambling around on the ground. It held a large nut in its mouth and, while nervously looking over its shoulder, scraped at the earth and then used its small fists to pound the nut into a shallow hole. It was the first bone-chilling day of fall, cold and windy. Knowing that food would soon be in short supply, the squirrel was preparing for winter by caching whatever provisions it could find. I felt a kinship with the squirrel and could identify with what it was doing.

The feeling is natural; we all require food, shelter and protection from our natural enemies. One of the activities shared by animals and humans is building. Humans construct dwellings, bridges, roads and waterways. Our houses protect us from the sun, wind, rain and cold. Our transportation routes make travel speedy and safe. Because we are able to modify our environment to serve our needs, we can live almost anywhere on Earth.

Animals also build a variety of structures, including shelters to protect themselves and their offspring and runways to make fast tracks to their food sources. Many animals construct traps that help them collect food. Some whales blow a curtain of bubbles that works like a net to surround and confuse their prey. From the spiderweb to the beaver lodge, animals have devised architectural solutions to specific problems and needs. In many ways, animals modify their environments in order to survive.

But unlike humans, animals do not work from a plan, and they do not have the benefit of tools. They have no cranes, drills or power machinery — not even hammers and nails. Their sharp teeth, beaks and dexterous claws and feet are the only tools they have with which to transport and manipulate the materials they use.

Building materials must be fashioned from the resources found in nature. The materials some creatures use in construction come from their own body fluids. Others invent new ways to use available materials. Mud, for instance, becomes mortar when mixed with grass or straw. The leaves of large plants are roofing shingles. Moss or cattail down can be insulation or perhaps bedding.

Whether we realize it or not, many of our activities and the patterns of our way of living come from those that were established in nature millions of years ago. The fluffy insulation of mouse and bird nests performs the same function as the insulation fibres that we use to keep our houses warm. Wasps and ants design their colonies with central heating, cooling and ventilation systems. Hornets, mixing wood and water, invented paper long before humans did. Burrowing mammals cache their winter supply of food in the ground in the same way that people store their fruit and root

crops inside cool, dark cellars.

In this book, we are going to look at one aspect of design in nature: animal architecture. We will see how and why animals build different structures. We will learn that the architecture of animals reveals a great deal about their nature, their behaviour, their needs and their solutions to problems that might threaten their survival. As we become aware of how animals build, we also begin to realize that human architects constantly reproduce images that already exist in nature. Animals have developed impressive answers to questions about insulation, solar heat, ventilation, drainage and waterproofing — precisely the same construction problems faced by humans.

Aggressively territorial, muskrats bond during the breeding season and may produce two to three litters per year, each containing up to 12 offspring. Born blind and completely dependent on the adults, the young are weaned within a month and reach maturity after six months. Muskrats are preyed upon by many other animals, and they are often victims of attack by their own species. Females will attempt to seize another muskrat's burrow by killing the resident and its offspring. Nesting females must fight off such intruders. Although male partners provide little care for the young, they will protect them from attack.

Each of us has come back from a day at the beach carrying a bag filled with shells. It is almost impossible to walk along the miles of sand and not stop to collect or examine what has washed ashore. Smooth, colourful and elegantly shaped, shells are a kind of treasure waiting to be discovered.

Like empty bird nests, such shells are the abandoned houses of living creatures. But a mollusk's shell is a living architecture.

The texture and the consistency of the shell provide clues about the life history of its inhabitant. Fast-moving currents keep shells smooth, while shells with a rough texture or with external growths are found in slow-moving or still waters. Holes, cracks and scars are the telltale signs of attacks by predators.

The mollusk is an invertebrate. It lacks bones and has a soft, unsegmented body. The mollusk's shell creates a bony structure on the outside of the body, rather than on the inside. It is the animal's armour, protecting the fleshy body from predators, and without it, the mollusk is relatively defenceless. The mollusk lives, feeds, reproduces and moves in its shell.

SNAILS & CLAMS

Mollusk shells are made from a mineral compound called calcium carbonate. Even the fossil remains of shells are mainly made of this substance. Calcium carbonate is also an important part of our bones, and in a soft form, it is used as chalk. It is a chief ingredient in the limestone we use to construct houses and other buildings. Humans cut limestone blocks out of the earth, but mollusks obtain calcium carbonate in a dissolved form through the water or soil they live in. Then the animal secretes, or releases, the calcified shell material from the mantle, a fleshy pouch that covers its internal organs, and begins to build its own home.

The clam is known as a bivalve because its shell looks as though it has two separate parts; in fact, the shell is a single unit divided by a ligament, which is made of a less concentrated form of calcium carbonate. The clam's symmetrical shell completely encases and protects the animal but also severely limits the clam's movement. By opening its valves slightly and extending a muscular foot, the clam drags itself through the sand, leaving a meandering trail on the lake bottom. When closed, the shell is clamped tightly by the hinge ligament, which is connected to the largest muscle in the clam's body.

To take advantage of the limita-

The spiral pattern of growth on the snail shell, previous and facing pages, is designed for strength. New material is added to the shell from the lip of the mantle, a point on the shell that is closest to the body. As the spiral winds around itself, the shell is constantly being reinforced from the outside. The bivalve, above, is kept secure by the muscular hinge ligament that clamps the shell tightly shut. The rings of growth are smaller, tighter and more concentrated at the ligament than they are anywhere else on the shell.

tions imposed by its shell and its watery habitat, the clam has devised a foraging technique known as filter feeding. Its gills are covered with fine hairs called cilia that beat like a rotating belt, washing water over the gills and filtering out organisms that are then passed forward to the clam's mouth.

The benefits of living in a clamshell are offset by a major disadvantage: the inhabitant is a virtual prisoner in its own home. It cannot run away from danger. Parasites silently bore through the exteriors and devour the inhabitants, while birds smash the casings by dropping them on rocks, and muskrats regularly feed on clams by forcing them open. Starfish digest clams by pushing their own stomachs between the valves, and drill snails make neat holes in the shells of other mollusks with their rasping tongues.

Some shells are better suited for a mobile life. A snail moves around far more easily than a clam does. Carrying its shell on its back, it inches along by extending and contracting the muscular foot located on the underside of its body. The snail has better-developed sensory organs than the clam. As a land mollusk, the garden snail has a tooth that scrapes plant tissue for food.

The snail shell spirals from left to right, a pattern set by the growth of the snail's internal organs during the larval stage. As the body begins to twist, the shell starts as a calcified cap that grows on the snail's back.

By the time the twisting is complete, the organs are repositioned to allow the snail to withdraw its head first and use its foot as a protective plug. The shell retains moisture; in dry or cold weather and in extreme conditions, the snail creates a limestone plug to seal the opening.

Shells come in a great variety of shapes and colours, but all of the more than 50,000 mollusk species share similar structures and methods of shell production. Some are covered with protective spines; others are built stronger for life in the pounding surf; some are constructed for digging through mud; and yet others are like bowls that clamp securely onto rocks. As you look at each one, remember that every shell is a record of a unique way of living.

Mollusks are a perfect marriage of architecture and life. The soft-bodied mollusk cannot survive without its shell, and as the mollusk grows, so does the shell. An empty shell is the abandoned home of a living creature, and it provides clues about the former occupant. Scars and cracks in the surface tell of predatory attacks, and the texture of the shell reveals the mollusk's environment. In fact, the shell tells us everything there is to know about the inhabitant: its species, its age, where it lived and its health. But unlike the architecture of other creatures, molluskan architecture is not a deliberate construction by the animal; rather, it is living architecture secreted by an animal's body.

Most of us have a love-hate relationship with insects and spiders. Some of them, like hornets, sting viciously. Cockroaches disgust us when we find them in our kitchen cupboards. The thought of tarantulas terrifies us, yet butterflies are beautiful to everyone.

Few animals build more impressively than insects do. Colonies of social insects such as ants and bees have often been compared to human cities. Such insects construct condominium-style complexes that are well organized and complete with special storage facilities, ventilation, entrances and exits.

Bee and wasp societies have developed unique and practical building materials. Wasps have invented strong, water-resistant paper that is so lightweight, the insects can easily position their nests in safe places. To keep the paper houses warm, wasps have devised central heating.

Humans are still trying to duplicate the silk and the incredibly complex engineering feat of the spider's suspended web. The net of the caddis fly and the circular web, or orb, of the spider are like giant fishing nets that locate and trap prey. Mound ants developed the original solar house.

We can learn much from the structures produced by insects and spiders in their independent and busy world. Long before humans evolved, insects were building elegant solutions to age-old problems.

The orb-weaving spider, previous page, positions its web where it can trap flying insects. Carpenter ant galleries, top, are lines chewed in the trunks of decaying trees. Members of the carpenter ant colony, bottom, feed and clean the eggs and helpless larvae.

CARPENTER & OTHER ANTS

By the time you see carpenter ants in your home, the black large-bodied insects have probably already begun to carve their way through the structure of your house, undoing the work of human carpenters.

All ant societies are social. Based on a caste system, they consist of queens, drones, workers and soldiers. The queen, which can live for up to 15 years, starts out alone and cares for the first brood without the help of workers. The carpenter queen selects a suitable log or tree in which to carve out a nesting chamber where she will lay her eggs. Secluded in the chamber, the queen relies on the energy stores in her system to sustain her; occasionally, she eats one of her own eggs. She feeds the larvae from her salivary glands.

As soon as the first brood pupates, the newly emerged workers become round-the-clock caretakers, licking and cleaning the remaining eggs to prevent decay. The queen then spends all her time laying eggs. When the larvae have hatched, the workers bring them food. The workers also move the larvae from one cavity to the next to ensure that they are warm and dry.

Carpenter ants build a labyrinth of chambers to house their growing colony. The tunnels, or galleries, they dig contain many similar chambers; some are reserved for nesting, while others are used for food storage. Each season, the queen lays unfertilized eggs that hatch only males. At the same time, she lays other eggs that become the next winged females to go out and establish new colonies.

Rather than eating wood, carpenter ants simply chew it up as they excavate galleries in the beams of houses. In live trees, they dig their galleries by following the concentric rings or longitudinal grain of the tree and burrowing through the soft cambium layer. The carpenter ant colony grows continually and is restricted only by the size of the tree it inhabits.

Once they burrow into the protection of a house beam, carpenter ants face few predators. However, in the wild, birds such as the pileated woodpecker work hard to pry them out of their galleries and feed on them, and insect-eating animals like bears tear trees open to get at the larvae and pupae – if they pick the right tree, they could stumble on a cache of thousands. On your next walk through the woods, look for the large black ants on rotten trees.

Some ants build domed and thatched mounds that serve as warm, dry incubators for pupae. Other species construct nests of a papery material chewed from plant debris and glued to rocks and tree trunks. Some hollow out underground chambers around plant

roots and use them to grow aphids –
insects that feed on plant sap and
produce nectar for the ants to eat.

Other kinds of ants build in the
soil. Their colonies possess the same
basic interior chambers as those
built in wood, and the colony grows
in much the same way. They can be
seen almost anywhere on a city
sidewalk. When you sweep the surface sand away, there appears to be
nothing underneath.

Ants mix and move a lot of soil,
and that helps to keep it loose and
absorbent. In spite of the annoyance
we feel at the sight of ants at a pic-
nic or in the countless other places
they appear, they do their share to
make the planet habitable. Not only
do ants improve the quality of our
soil, but their diet includes many insects that are harmful to humans.
Up to 100,000 insects can be captured by one colony in a single day.

Beneath an exterior mound of pine
needles, leaves and grass, the ant colony
is constructed vertically in the soil.
Because it is not defined by a limited
space, the ant colony can continue to
grow, with underground galleries for
nesting, raising offspring and storing
food. To keep the colony dry, the
workers continually rotate moist and
musty grains of soil from interior
chambers to the outside.

13

The potter wasp makes an individual clay pot for each of its eggs. The opening of the nest is so tiny that the female must force the food—stunned beetle grubs—through it before she deposits the egg. The potter wasp is the only species that suspends its egg from the opening of the nesting pot on a strand of sticky material. Once the egg hatches, the larva feeds on the stored grubs. The greatest danger to the larva may be its close quarters. The potter wasp's sting often sedates its prey only temporarily, leaving the egg or larva at risk of being crushed by wriggling grubs.

Rather than excavating a nesting cavity, the leaf-cutter bee deposits its eggs individually in snail shells, hollow branches, worm holes and the galleries of wood-boring insects. It lines the nesting chamber with leaf cuttings, which act as a vapour barrier, and stocks the cavity with beebread to feed the larva.

SOLITARY BEES & WASPS

Solitary bees and wasps provide their offspring with a peaceful existence compared with the chaotic life of insects in a large society. In the social colony, the queen's only job is to lay eggs, and she relies on the help of thousands of workers to do the rest of the work. Unlike the social queen, the solitary female bee or wasp works entirely on her own to lay the eggs, build the nest and feed the offspring. She provides everything that will allow the eggs to develop into adults.

The greatest dangers facing the larvae of solitary bees are mould and decay. Each species has its own solution. Some line the cavities with an absorbent paper, others create a vapour barrier to keep out moisture by covering the cell walls with a waxy resin.

To line the interior of her nest, the female leaf-cutter bee chews a bite-sized track in a green leaf, rolls it up like a tiny carpet and carries it back to the nest. She places a number of these in the nesting chamber – usually an insect hole bored in a tree stump. Collecting circular pieces of leaves, she caps the bottom of the tubes already shoved down the hole. In sequence, she lays an egg in each cavity, fills the tube with beebread – a cakelike substance of nectar and pollen – and seals it with a piece of leaf. When the chamber is full, she packs the remaining space with insulating leaf pieces, plugging the entranceway.

Unlike vegetarian bees, wasps are carnivorous; their food ranges from caterpillars to the larvae of beetles and flies. Some species practise what is known as mass provisioning: they stock the nest with all the food that the offspring will require to grow into an adult. There is a risk involved in placing an egg in a confined space with beetles and flies that are simply sedated, however; upon awakening, the insects could easily crush the fragile egg.

The female potter wasp fashions pots of clay to house her eggs. She kneads the clay with her mandibles and front legs until it is the correct texture, adding water when necessary. Carrying the pellets to the building site one by one, she constructs the hollow sphere, flattening the pellets to form the exterior.

After the pot is completed, the wasp collects enough beetle larvae to allow her to feed her offspring until it pupates. Although unable to fit through the narrow neck of the pot herself, she forces the stunned prey inside. As she lays the egg, she secretes a strand of sticky fluid that suspends it safely above the paralyzed prey.

The thread-waisted wasp protects its eggs from the dangers of being crushed by providing food gradually. The wasp digs a vertical shaft in the sand with her front legs and her mandibles, carting away the

loosened soil under her chin. To secure the nest, she seals each hole with a carefully chosen pebble, matching the opening of the nest by measuring it with her jaws.

After completing the nest, the female lays an egg directly on top of a stunned caterpillar, which she has dragged back to the nest. Although the female then leaves the nest and barricades the opening with a pebble, she checks the nest on a daily basis, providing the necessary food. It is only in the final days when her larva is sufficiently large and its survival assured that the female fills the cavity with caterpillars and seals the chamber. When the well-fed larva pupates, it digs its way out of the nest chamber, forces the barrier aside and emerges as an adult.

The sand wasp can be found on beaches or sand dunes. Using its front legs, it can excavate a nesting cavity in less than an hour; it then places its egg and food for its larva—stunned flies—inside the cavity. The wasp relies on landmarks in the surrounding area to indicate the location of its nest.

LARVAL ARCHITECTS

Some caddis flies cover their pupal chambers with twigs, stones or shells—whatever will make them look like natural parts of the environment. Every freshwater stream and pond is home to one of the numerous species of caddis fly. Using its sharp jaws and strong legs, the larva cuts and arranges the material on the exterior of the casing. After the larva pupates, it uses its mandibles to chew its way out of the protective tube.

For some insects, the larval stage of development is an active one, unlike the helpless state of grubs that rely on care provided by a colony. Caddis flies, ant lions and tent caterpillars provide for themselves. Completely independent, they build cocoons and trap the food necessary for their growth into adults.

The caddis fly is a master of disguise. Lying motionless at the edge of a stream, the caterpillarlike larva of the caddis moth lives in a silk tube spun from salivary material. The casing is carefully camouflaged and difficult to detect. Using its legs and sharp jaws, the larva cuts and arranges material on the outside of the casing. Some cover the tube with stones, twigs and shredded plants. Others use tiny snail shells or gravel and sand. If the species lives near fast-moving water, the larva anchors the casing with stones. As it grows, so does its sheath, and the larva moves around with its portable home on its back.

Positioned in or near the edge of the stream to allow water to circulate through it, the casing acts as a filter for bits of plant matter that the larva feeds on. When it is about to change into a winged adult, the larva seals the end of the tube with a covering that allows water to flow through, providing it with oxygen.

The larva of another species of caddis fly is a caterpillar that uses salivary material to spin a loose bag-like net to capture its food. The net is attached to a plant stem below the water's surface; the running water keeps the net inflated. The caterpillar hides in the neck of the bag, waiting to feed on whatever becomes trapped at the bottom. It is easy to find both species along the shores and in the shallow waters of slow-moving streams.

The ant lion larva traps its food in a cone-shaped pit it digs in the sand. It emerges from its hiding place beneath the hot sand, its pincerlike jaws straining wide, eager for its first meal of the day – perhaps a large black ant. The sides of the pit are steep, and the dry sand is loose. When the victim falls into the funnel, the ant lion flicks sand onto the sides of the pit to start an avalanche, knocking its prey within reach.

It eats by squirting fluids into the body of its prey and then sucking out the nutritious predigested portion. After eating, it tosses the indigestible shells out of the pit, leaving them to litter the exterior. The collection of body husks around the rim of the pit reveals what the ant lion has devoured.

Ant lions are easy to find on dry sand dunes or under porches. If you partially fill a glass jar with sand and place an ant lion inside, it will dig a pit. You can feed it a few ants every day to keep it satisfied.

In the tent caterpillar's larval stage, the offspring weave a tent for

16

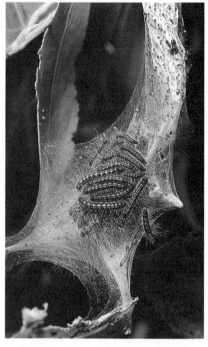

their home, usually on an apple or a cherry tree. Pitching a tent requires teamwork, and living in a family of a hundred or more, the tent caterpillar has lots of help. The tent is made of silk spun from special glands. Until they pupate and turn into brown moths, the caterpillars live in sheltered safety, protected from parasitic flies, ants, wasps and birds.

The tent looks like a net of pale white silk laced around the fork of a tree. Occasionally, the caterpillars leave the tent to sun themselves. They sometimes lay silk trails to feeding areas, which provide them with a secure grip on windy days.

Pivoting on its end like a drill, the ant lion larva creates a cone-shaped pit, above, 1½ inches deep in clean, dry sand. The sides of the trap are steep, and the sand is loose. If an ant steps on the rim of the funnel, the ant lion flicks sand onto the sides to start an avalanche. The ant lion, inset, is an insect possessed: the more it eats, the faster it becomes a winged adult moth. In its larval stage, it conceals itself beneath the surface of the sand with only its pincerlike jaws protruding, awaiting the arrival of its prey.

On a sunny day, these tiny tent caterpillars leave the safety of their home nest to float through the air on silk lines, venturing out to feed on a nearby fruit tree. During the larval stage, tent caterpillars nest as a family. When they are ready to pupate, they spin individual cocoons under rocks or in other well-protected areas, sometimes grouping together.

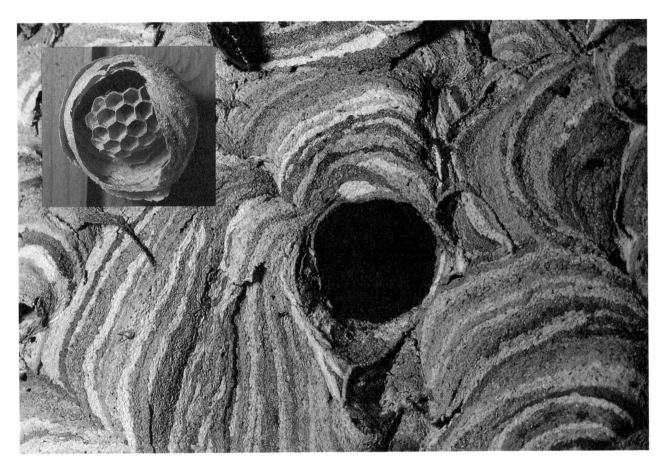

The shades and textures of finished wasp paper, above, reflect the variety of materials used to produce it. The paper is made by mixing saliva with fibres scraped from trees, dry grasses, fenceposts, cardboard and weather-beaten wood. As the colony grows, the nest expands vertically and laterally. Storeys are added from the top downward by means of columns that separate each level. No matter how large the nest becomes—some house thousands of individuals—a single flight hole is the only entrance, making defence against attacks from ants and other wasps easy. The common wasp's comb, inset, shows the first set of hexagonal (six-sided) cells. This nest, containing one unit, is that of a beginner, but as the colony grows, other layers of combs will be added, with the cells opening on the underside. The outer shell is built in layered sheets, and an insulating airspace is left in between. Eventually, the outer layer is completed, and the nest is closed.

SOCIAL BEES & WASPS

The low rumbling hum from a colony of bees or wasps is an ominous sound, like that of an impending invasion. What we are hearing, however, is the whirring of tens of thousands of dedicated workers either flying to and from the nest or ventilating it with their wings.

Paper-wasp nests are formed from a material that is warm, economical to produce, easy to use and waterproof. It is paper, made from pulp that the wasps create from wood shaved off a weather-beaten fencepost or a dying tree and mixed with their saliva to make it cohesive and water-repellent.

The queen begins the construction of the paper colony by building her first nest, a small comb of nesting chambers. It is attached by a stem to a secure, protected surface such as an overhanging rock or eave. The chambers open on the bottom and are covered with an envelope of paper; a single flight hole is left for an entrance. Later, the wasps alert one another to an attack by drumming on the walls.

As the colony grows, so does the nest. It is expanded in all directions. New storeys are added from the top downward. The paper envelope, which covers the nest cells, is layered in thin sheets, with a pocket of air between each layer. The wasps create the sheets by walking

A wasp collects fibres by walking backward and using its jaws like a wood shaver to pare long strips from the surface. To make paper, the wasp chews the dry material with its mandibles, mixing it with saliva. Back at the nest, it spreads the pulpy building material into a hexagonal structure, all the while straddling the wall or surface that it is working on. The hexagon is the strongest shape in nature and requires less material to construct. It begins as a round cell and takes on its form from the pressure of adjacent walls as additional cells are added to the exterior.

Labour in the honeybee colony is divided according to age. For the first few days of its life, a worker bee cleans the comb. Soon after, its glands begin to produce bee milk, which is fed to the larvae. Next, its wax glands become active, and the bee works full-time on construction. After the wax glands cease to function, the bee becomes an inside courier, transporting nectar and pollen for storage in the interior wax cells. Then the worker bee is a soldier, defending the stock of the colony—the larvae, the nectar and the honey—that attracts intruders. Its last weeks are spent in the field, gathering pollen and nectar, a job that involves the greatest number of risks.

backward and spreading the pulpy material with their mouths until it is flat. All the wood fibres in the nest are aligned in one direction, side by side, in order to give the structure greater strength.

The social wasps have a primitive but effective central heating system. Some workers generate heat for the nest with their own bodies. They keep the temperature at 86 degrees F. Warmer temperatures speed up larval growth. But if the temperature gets too high, workers leave the nest and bring back water to splash on the walls, fanning them with their wings to make it cooler inside.

Like the wasp nest, a honeycomb is started at the top. It has a central wall, from top to bottom, with cells on both sides. The bees conceal all seams, and the finished comb is very smooth. Although constantly stopping and starting, replacing one another and helping each other out, the bees know exactly what to do at each stage.

Another engineering feature shared by bees and wasps is the shape of the cells, which are used to raise the young and to store food. The six-sided chamber, or hexagon, provides a lot of storage space but requires little room or materials. Shapes like the triangle and the square are bigger on the outside, and therefore, more materials would be needed to build them. With the hexagonal cells, the sides that are joined together not only save mate-

rials but provide additional strength. Angled slightly to prevent the stored pollen from running out, the cells open at the front. Cells that contain honey or a pupating grub are closed with a protective cover.

Honeybees use a special building material—wax—that is produced by glands on the underside of the worker's body. First, the bees join together in a chain. Then they curl into a ball, generating a temperature of 95 degrees F. Wax begins to appear as tiny flakes on each bee's abdomen. It is scraped off with a hind leg and passed to the front legs and mandibles. The bee kneads and mixes the wax with saliva until it is soft enough to be worked.

When constructing the comb, the bee uses the tips of its touch-sensitive antennae to ensure a consistent thickness in the cell walls. Because the wax is soft and warm when it is applied, it can be squeezed. The bee pushes the wax with its bristles. The length of time it takes for the wax to pop back enables the bee to gauge the thickness of the wall. Its head functions as a sort of living plumb line, helping it to keep the lines of construction true.

Bee's glue, called propolis, is a mixture of plant resin and saliva. Bees gnaw at sticky buds, sap ooze and bark, collecting resin and carrying it home in "buckets" on their hind legs. People use propolis to make high-quality varnish for violins and other fine wood products. Some bees in very warm climates

mix their glue with the wax. The comb can then withstand hotter temperatures without melting.

The honeybee nest is a remarkable structure. It enables the bees to remain cool in summer and warm in bad weather. It provides shelter for the colony, nesting chambers for the developing offspring and a convenient storage area for surplus food. Humans the world over work to enjoy similar comforts.

The honeycomb is a factory of uniformly organized cells that must continue to produce new workers to carry on the colony. Breeding cells are covered with a dome of wax during pupation. Elsewhere in the comb, storage cells—for pollen and honey—remain uncapped; the largest cells are reserved for breeding queens and drones. Larval cells are also kept open while the larvae are dependent on food provided by young workers.

21

ORB-WEAVING SPIDERS

The spider's orb works like a giant net. Whether the spider is active or not, the web continues to act as a trap for food. From the centre of its web, the spider can, by using the "telegraph wire," determine when prey touches the web. But the web is not foolproof.

Sometimes, larger flying insects trap the spider by presenting themselves in the web as prey. When the spider closes in to sting its "victim," the insect devours it and then flies free, too heavy to be ensnared by the web.

Accidentally walking into a spider-web will give you some quick lessons on the basic properties of spider silk, which is almost impossible to see with the naked eye. Most visible strands are multiples – four or five filaments joined together. A single strand can be as small as one-millionth of an inch in diameter; the thickest is only four times that size.

You cannot shake the feeling that it is stuck all over you. That is because the strands are amazingly elastic; they can stretch to twice their length without breaking. Spider silk is the strongest material in the world, stronger than steel of the same thickness. A liquid protein, silk is produced by glands in the spider's abdomen. As it is squeezed out of the spinnerets at the rear of its body, the protein hardens.

A set of woven silk strands, the web is designed to trap insects and to provide a dwelling for the spider; it also enables the spider to feed on insects that are too difficult to stalk. Its design is based on the same principle that humans use to build a suspension bridge. The strands are organized in a complex network of tensions that keeps the entire orb taut and in place. Flexible and light, the web is strong enough to hold struggling insects.

The orb web is a lopsided circle constructed around a Y-frame called the first fork. The number of spokes varies, but few orbs have more than 50. The spider fills in the largest gaps first by measuring them with its legs while standing at the hub. By the time the outer rim and the spokes are completed, the frame has been transformed from a Y to a tilted wheel solidly anchored at several points.

The rim of the orb is made by pacing the edge of the frame. The spokes are joined with a temporary dry spiral of silk. Then, starting from the centre, the spider moves to the outside of the web, weaving a tight spiral of sticky threads that increase the tension. The spider snaps each line before attaching it, which separates the sticky solution into beads that dot the strand.

When a flying insect gets caught in the lines, the spider feeds by injecting it with poison and sucking out its insides, or the spider may, instead, bind the victim in silk and store it to eat later. To avoid sticking to its own web, the orb weaver has developed feet that possess an extra claw and hairs with which it grasps the silk thread. Newly hatched spiders feed on the digestible pollen that blows onto the web and sticks there.

But not all spiders spin webs, and not all web-spinning spiders make orbs. Spiders that eat flying insects create orbs. Others make horizontal hammock-style webs which trap insects that walk or hop.

All the information a spider needs

to know about the position of food in the web and about maintaining the web is transmitted through its legs. The web has a "telegraph wire." From the centre of the orb, the spider uses its legs to "listen" to the telegraph wire to determine when the web has been touched and when it might be holding a victim. Even if the prey is motionless, the spider can pinpoint it by plucking the strands, a method that is also used to detect breaks in the orb.

If you trap a spider in a shoebox or in a sheltered area like a porch, you may have a chance to observe the entire construction of a web. To see the detail, blow a light dusting of cornstarch or flour onto the web; outdoors, look early in the morning before the dew has dried.

Spider eggs are almost always laid in a mass and enclosed in a silk casing. Most spiders have a special set of glands that secrete the silk. The quantity of eggs and the extra care taken in protecting them improve the spiders' chances of survival. Many orb weavers deposit their eggs on the orb so that when the offspring hatch, they can be guarded and fed by the adult. Some spiders carry the silk-encased eggs around with them wherever they go. Others lay their eggs on a leaf, fold the leaf over them and then spin silk around the whole structure. Still others deposit their eggs on vegetation, rocks and tree branches and cover them with sticky silk that keeps out both the elements and predators, such as parasitic flies.

Life began in water, and most living matter still contains water and depends on it. We cannot breathe or survive below the surface for long, yet we like to swim in water, we drink it, and we consider it to be one of our most vital resources. One of the problems animals face is maintaining the balance of water, oxygen and heat required for their eggs to develop. Aquatic animals like fish and turtles use a variety of methods to achieve the correct balance.

Fish have lots of water, but they must place their eggs where there is also plenty of oxygen. In the spring, trout and salmon deposit their eggs on shallow gravel bars in streams flowing with clean oxygen-rich water. Other fish attach their eggs to oxygen-producing plants or fan the eggs to renew the oxygen supply.

To protect the fragile eggs, many fish construct nests. Some are primitive saucers fanned into the floor of a lake. They are sometimes covered with weeds or gravel to increase their security. A few fish use aquatic plants to construct a bird-style nest underwater. Generally, the fish that spend a lot of energy creating protective nests and guarding the eggs and hatchlings have a high offspring-survival rate. Clearly, fish have a lot to gain by taking extra care.

When the ancestors of turtles crawled from the sea onto land, they became the first animals to create an egg able to develop out of water. Reptiles, the first fully terrestrial group of animals, produce hard-shelled eggs that protect an embryo encased in fluid, enabling the embryo to survive even though the egg is laid in a relatively dry place.

Although the land egg contains adequate moisture, it still requires heat in order to develop. But reptiles have a body temperature that varies according to the temperature around them. In other words, they are unable to produce enough consistent heat to keep their eggs warm. Therefore, turtles evolved an ingenious solution to their dilemma: they use the sun-heated soil and sand to warm their eggs.

TURTLES

If the turtle looks strangely pre-historic, it is because that is exactly what it is. Dating back 200 million years, the cumbersome animal is the longest-surviving reptilian species. All of its contemporaries are extinct, but the turtle has some-how managed to survive. Lacking natural enemies, it can go about its adult life undisturbed. Not so for the much-sought-after turtle eggs.

Some mammals love to gorge themselves on turtle eggs. Raccoons and skunks stalk adult spotted and painted turtles as the slow-moving reptiles choose their nesting sites, then come back later to unearth and feast upon the tender eggs. In the Tropics, the coatimundi – a masked, ring-tailed monkeylike relative of the raccoon – raids the beaches dur-ing the egg-laying season in search of the nests of the spectacular sea turtle. One of the turtle's challenges, then, has been how to conceal the eggs until they hatch; after that, it is up to the hatchlings.

The turtle has one of the most cu-rious reproductive patterns of any reptile. Able to live out of water – partly because of its leathery skin, which seals in moisture that would otherwise be lost to the air – it lays eggs on land even though it lives in a watery habitat. Each season, the turtle has to find a suitable land lo-cation to use to deposit its eggs.

The slow current of a shallow stream, previous page, provides ideal conditions for the stickleback nest. Fish eggs need plenty of fresh water in order to develop. As long as water washes over the nest, the eggs will receive adequate oxygen, and silt and fungus will not collect on them. Equipped with strong, clawed legs, the snapping turtle, above, crawls over irregular swampy terrain in search of soft, sandy soil that will make a suitable site for its nest.

Wearing its bony box on its back, the turtle is self-contained, protected and able to travel outside its normal habitat to a nesting site. The shell is not only the turtle's portable house but also its expanded external rib cage, which shields the lungs that enable it to breathe air and to survive on land.

Because the turtle is cold-blooded, it cannot incubate and hatch eggs with its own body. Its solution is to dig holes in the sand in which it buries the eggs so that they are warm enough to develop and safe from predators. The architecture is simple, but it does the job: the soil where the eggs are buried collects the warmth from the sun, storing it and incubating the eggs.

The female snapping turtle crawls onto shore in spring or summer and digs a pit in loose soil on a sunny slope. Using her hind feet, she shovels out a hole into which she deposits about two dozen eggs. Because so many predators like to eat their eggs, turtles do what they can to avoid being seen when they lay them.

Turtle eggs have hard shells compared with the eggs of a fish or an amphibian, which must be bathed in moisture to keep them from drying out. Yet they are not brittle like bird eggs. Their rubbery texture makes them more like shell-less hard-boiled eggs, enabling them to be dropped into the bottom of the pit without cracking. If the turtle can dig a pit with a gravelly bottom,

the nest will have natural drainage and the eggs will not rot.

Once the pit is dug and the eggs are incubating, the female's job is done. Beyond building a well-drained nest in a location hidden from predators, the female takes no further care of the offspring. When the first egg begins to crack from the scratching of the turtle inside, it is a signal to the other hatchlings to start coming out of their shells. After hatching, they move upward together in relays, some digging while others rest. Upon reaching the surface, the offspring are on their own and quickly make their way toward the nearby water, virtually running for their lives. Many are captured by gulls and owls during their desperate flight to safety.

The egg-laying season for the snapping turtle begins in June and lasts until the middle of July. The female digs one nest per season into which she deposits her eggs, which hatch in late summer or early fall. The sound of the first turtle breaking out of its shell signals the other hatchlings to do the same, and then together, they claw their way to the surface. Newborn turtles are wrinkled and dark and have soft shells. Adult snapping turtles are carnivorous, feeding on fish, frogs, insects, crustaceans and young waterfowl, but the snapper starts its life on a diet of vegetation.

The male pumpkinseed, a member of the sunfish family, constructs his nest in shallow areas with underwater vegetation. The pumpkinseed grows up to nine inches in length. The male uses his powerful tail fin to fan the nesting site clear of loose vegetation and mud, exposing the hard bottom of the lake or pond. In a prime nesting area—weedy and warm—pumpkinseeds build their nests in colonies, spaced three feet apart and visible for as far as the eye can see.

PUMPKINSEED SUNFISH

With its golden brown flanks and head and shimmering highlights of olive, orange, red, blue and green, the pumpkinseed is one of North America's most beautiful sunfish. In the South, it is called a panfish because it is round and flat—just the right shape for a frying pan.

Found in small lakes, ponds and other clear waters with underwater vegetation, the pumpkinseed can be seen in nearly all freshwater locations in eastern Canada, with the highest concentrations in the St. Lawrence River, its connecting streams and lakes and in some of the Great Lakes. It has a general diet and feeds on dragonfly nymphs, ants, larval salamanders, worms, snails, insect larvae and the hatchlings of other fish species.

The pumpkinseed builds a saucer-shaped nest in late spring or early summer, once its spawning season begins. Depending on the temperature, the season can last through to late summer. With its fins, the male fans a shallow depression in the floor of a lake or river. The diameter of the nest is usually twice the length of the fish that builds it. As with many other species, the male pumpkinseed constructs the nest near the shore on the gravelly bottom of slow-moving waters.

The male entices the female to the nesting site by moving in circles around her. While swimming over the area of the nest, the male and female prod and butt one another to stimulate the spawn. The male remains in an upright position during the spawn, and the female slants her body at an angle of 45 degrees. With their bellies, or ventral sides, facing, they release small quantities of eggs and sperm at intervals, and the fertilized eggs stick in clumps to the vegetation in the nest.

Staying near the nest during the three-day incubation period, the male pumpkinseed fans it with his tail to increase the supply of oxygen flowing over the eggs, aiding their development and preventing fungal growth. For the next 10 exhausting days, the male remains with the hatchlings. With thousands of babies to watch over, the male is very busy protecting them from bullheads and bass.

He gets some help from the chain pickerel, a species that has been observed patrolling nearby like a watchdog, feeding on the golden shiners that have developed a taste for pumpkinseed eggs. After the pumpkinseed fry leave the nest, the male cleans it for the next generation; if the weather stays warm, spawning may occur several times.

In May or June, if you row a boat out to the shallows where the wind and waves keep the weeds down flat, you will see male pumpkinseeds dutifully guarding their nests. Better yet, put on a mask and snorkel, and watch the beautiful pumpkinseeds at close range.

Stationing himself over the nest, the male pumpkinseed protects the eggs. If the temperature is more than 80 degrees F, the eggs hatch in as little as three days. In order to fill the nest, the male may bring more than one female to lay eggs. The male then has his work cut out for him: since each female can lay up to 5,000 eggs, the male may have to guard as many as 15,000 hatchlings. Nothing can distract him from his job as guardian. He stays with the babies, chasing away larger predatory species and retrieving offspring that stray from the nest. After 10 days, the young leave the nest for good, and the male cleans it in preparation for another spawning.

THREE-SPINED STICKLEBACKS

The tiny fish gets its ferocious-sounding name from the three sharp spines on its dorsal side. Each one looks like a tiny sail and has a soft triangular membrane. Armoured with bony plates instead of scales, the three-spined stickleback varies in colour from a silvery green to olive, with dark markings. Its fins are pale but, during mating season, may look red. Although the stickleback is only two inches long, it provides an impressive display of building and parental care.

In the spring, rising water temperatures signal the male stickleback that it is time to spawn. In warmer places, spawning begins as early as April, and in colder regions, it can go on as late as September. The male moves into the shallow water of sandy-bottomed rivers and lakes and, sweeping vigorously with its fins, clears away any loose weeds from its chosen site. It then starts to gather the material it needs to construct a nest, carrying plant debris, small twigs, seaweed and bits of algae in its mouth and piling them together in a barrel shape.

Then the male swims back and forth over the nest, secretes a sticky substance that hardens when it comes into contact with water and glues the nesting material together. Next, the stickleback excavates a tunnel through the pile of twigs.

The stickleback spawn is orchestrated by a series of signals. During the mating season, the male and female stickleback change in appearance to help members of the species recognize each other. The spinal membranes, chest and belly of the male, which are normally greenish in colour, become brilliant red. The throat and belly of the female turn pinkish. When the partners approach the nest, the male encourages the female to go into the tunnel by swimming around and through the nest. Once the female enters, the male stickleback prods her to stimulate the release of eggs. When the female is finished, the male chases her away, then fertilizes the eggs.

Swimming in a zigzag pattern, the male invites a female to follow him to the nesting site. An interested female approaches the male with her head held up. The male circles the nest and nudges the female, encouraging her to enter. After she does, the male prods her tail, causing her to release her eggs. When the female leaves the tunnel, the male chases her away and enters the nesting cavity to fertilize the eggs.

The spawning complete, the male makes any necessary repairs to the nest. He loosens the roof material to increase water circulation and cleans the nest of any egg casings that, when they rot, might affect the fertilized eggs. Every once in a while, the male fans the tunnel to provide oxygen for the eggs.

The eggs hatch in about seven days, and the male watches over the small fish, or fry, retrieving any that stray. But after about two weeks, the energetic fry have reduced their nursery to a shambles and the nest is of no further use. The young venture into deeper water, and the male stickleback's job is over.

Like the pumpkinseed, the male stickleback may recruit more than one female to deposit eggs. As many as 600 eggs have been found in a three-spined stickleback's nest. The eggs, which stick together in clumps, are cloudy and yellowish in colour—the same colour as the hatchlings. During the seven-day incubation period, the male ventilates the nest by periodically fanning it with his front fins and cleans away egg casings or unfertilized eggs that could decay and thereby damage the unhatched eggs.

Whether wedged into the fork of a tree, woven between two bulrushes, firmly tied to the outermost tip of a branch or perched on a desert cactus, a bird nest is a finely crafted thing. With a minimum of tools – a sharp beak, keen vision and flexible feet – birds construct a variety of nests using twigs, grass, soil and leaves – whatever they can find in their territory.

Some species are weavers and have learned to tie and knot pliable grasses. Others work like masons, plastering their nests with mud. Some camouflage the exterior of the nests to match the surroundings.

Although there are as many different bird nests as there are species of birds, nests are built mainly as a place in which to lay and incubate eggs. Bird feathers work as an insulating layer to save energy and turn it into body heat, just as fur does for mammals. A stable, or constant, body temperature means that, unlike their reptilian ancestors, birds can incubate their eggs directly, which is a safer, faster method for hatching the young.

But nesting and building are not always the same thing. Many birds lay their eggs in unconstructed nests – a primitive scrape in the ground, for instance. Others enjoy the luxury of a constructed nest, but one that is not their own. They steal a nest from a hardworking builder and adapt it to their needs. Cowbirds sneak their eggs into another bird's nest, thereby freeing themselves of the work involved in raising their own young.

Flight allows many birds to locate their nests at very high elevations, well hidden by leaves. But in the autumn, after the leaves have fallen, nests are easily seen. You can learn much about a bird's environment and its resourcefulness by carefully taking apart a bird nest to reveal the variety of materials that were painstakingly gathered to create it.

ORIOLES

The female oriole weaves a neat hanging basket for her offspring safely beyond the range of most predators. The pendulous nest is strong and secure; it is fashioned from native fibres and animal hair in a durable and tight weave. The female attaches the structure to the outermost limb of a tall tree, usually one that grows along the outskirts of a wooded area.

Construction of the nest is a real test of the oriole's coordination and stamina. It takes anywhere from 4 to 15 days to complete. To weave the nest, the female positions herself on the branch above and works upside down, lacing the surrounding branches with pliable strands of hemp. Then she interweaves dandelion and cattail down between the support strips to fill in the shape. The nest looks like a woollen ski tuque that found its way into the washing machine's hot cycle. The oriole's beak is similar to a darning needle: elongated and sharp but heavy enough to separate plant fibres into threads.

Soft and comfortable, the interior of the oriole's nest looks like a hammock and is lined with animal hair so neatly tied up that there are no loose ends or straggly pieces. While the oriole is weaving the nest, she periodically jumps inside to shape the bag and adjust the tension. The structure's only opening is at the

The young broad-tailed hummingbird, previous page, tests its wings in a behaviour called wing-fanning before embarking on its first flight. The nest it occupies is a deep cup woven into a frame of spider silk. One to two inches in diameter, it is made of bark, leaves and twigs, and the exterior is covered with lichens. It is positioned on the low branches of willows or cottonwoods. After they hatch, northern orioles, above, remain in the nest for about two weeks. During this time, both parents hunt for soft insects to feed the hungry hatchlings.

Birds are determined builders and, when necessary, can improvise building materials from whatever they find in their environment. Although the oriole prefers to construct its nest with milkweed fluff, hemp, pliable bark and animal hair, it will also use bits of cloth and string that are neatly woven into the hanging basket. A northern oriole has formed the basic structure of the nest shown above from nylon fishing line, although long strands are more difficult to manipulate and can pose some hazards during building. Orioles have been found strangled in unmanageable strands of building material.

top; the eggs and hatchlings sit well concealed in the bottom of the nest.

Hanging from the tip of the most delicate tree limbs, the basket is completely out of the reach of all predators except, perhaps, the snake. The nest, nevertheless, has certain limitations: it is vulnerable during windy weather, and it cannot be built in a closed or densely overgrown forest. This makes the oriole a forest-edge species.

The oriole does not begin nest construction until late in the season, when the leaves are on the trees, so the nests are sometimes difficult to spot. Leave oriole nesting material, such as string and thread, in your backyard, and the bird will visit regularly and make use of it. If you watch carefully when the bird carries away the string, you should be able to follow the oriole to its nesting site.

The female oriole may return to a favourite nesting tree year after year. Using her strong beak like a darning needle, she weaves together the strands of a variety of fibres. While the male guards against intruders from neighbouring trees, the female constructs the nest and incubates the eggs.

While the female short-billed marsh wren selects her nest from among the many decoy nests built by the male, the female long-billed marsh wren constructs her own. Large, round and covered, the woven nest is situated in the long grasses of the marsh. The elevated nest's side opening and roofed style of construction make it secure and dry. The outer walls are woven from strips of coarse, pliable marsh grasses, which give the nest a distinctly untidy look, while the more orderly interior walls are woven from finer grasses and lined with feathers and cattail down. The long-billed marsh wren raises two broods per season, with five or six eggs per brood; the female incubates the eggs for up to 16 days. The young leave the nest two weeks after hatching. The male may mate with several females in neighbouring territories.

MARSH WRENS

When young birds set out to build their first nests, they are completely on their own. They proceed by instinct, choosing site, nest style and materials; they do not receive instruction from their parents. In some cases, even though first-time builders may not possess the artistry of the seasoned adult, they know enough of the basics to get by. For others, it is a matter of "practice makes perfect." They find out very quickly whether or not they are doing the right thing. And if any bird has good reason to improve its building skills, it is the marsh wren.

The short-billed marsh, or sedge, wren common to the sedge meadows of North America constructs a covered nest. It is a well-hidden ball of woven dry and green grasses with the opening on the side—placed either one or two feet off the ground or in among the weeds and bulrushes. This style affords the wren greater protection and is a considerably more advanced design than the open, or cup-style, nest.

The building behaviour of the marsh wren is unique among songbirds. Not only does the nest serve as a place for the wren to roost and hatch its young, but it also attracts a mate. The male is the builder. He constructs several decoy nests—created to confuse predators—and uses them to lure females to him.

When he can, the male wren

takes more than one mate; the harder he works at nest building, sometimes producing up to 10 nests at a time, the more mates he can attract. It is a sign of his experience and skill if he can entice more than one. When a female approaches, the male runs in and out of each nest, subtly suggesting that the female enter. The female's choice of mate is based on the male's architectural talent. Her role in the nest building is a minor one—she lines the interior with feathers and plant down.

To attract a mate, the male long-billed marsh wren puffs out his chest feathers, cocks his tail and serenades from the top of a cattail stand. Only 4 to 5½ inches long, with a 5-to-7-inch wingspan, this small songbird spends the summer in the marshy meadows of North America. The wren's upper body is brown, with a streaked head and back and an identifying white stripe over each eye. Using its long, slim bill, the marsh wren eats spiders and a variety of insects and their larvae, including moths, mosquitoes and beetles.

The female robin weaves her elevated nest from grass and twigs on a foundation of mud. The robin may have three broods per season, each containing up to six eggs. Feeding hungry nestlings demands the hunting expertise of both parents. By the time the hatchlings are ready to leave the nest, each may have consumed as much as 200 feet of earthworms. They will still be wearing their juvenile brown-speckled plumage, which is similar to their thrush family relatives' and serves as useful camouflage for these inexperienced fliers. Sometimes, the male accompanies the young for a few days, acting as a bodyguard until they are able to manage for themselves.

ROBINS

For days before the female robin begins construction of the nest, she surveys her chosen tree. She twists and turns on a selection of branches as though she were checking the specifications. And that is precisely what she is doing. The female's body is the measure for the size and shape of the nest, so if the tree limb does not suit her, it will not be suitable for the nest. Moving from branch to branch, she views the tree from all angles, evaluating where best to place the foundation.

The robin's nest is one of the best built of all songbirds'. Each year, the robin returns to the same tree and may even reuse the solid mud foundation of an old nest. While most nests cannot be reused because they eventually become overrun with parasites, the robin has found a solution to the problem: she simply plasters nest parasites into the cup with mud.

A strong nest is a necessity for the robin because of the vulnerability of its offspring. Generally speaking, the more vulnerable and dependent the young, the more secure are the nests built by their parents. Hatching from blue eggs, robin nestlings are born helpless, blind, featherless and unable to stand; they require the safety of an elevated nest with high walls to keep them from falling out. The robin constructs a substantial bowl-shaped structure of

twigs, weed stems and grass on a mud base. The nest is lined with fine grasses and softer plant material; the female uses her chest to shape the bowl. The neat, deep cup is situated 5 to 20 feet above the ground where, saddled on a tree fork, it is sheltered from the rain.

One species that has benefited from the presence of humans, the robin is much more common in the city than in the forest, since finding food on the ground is difficult and dangerous in overgrown areas. And because it does so well in cities, the robin provides many people with their first glimpse of a bird nest and eggs. Few sights are more beautiful and memorable than the uniquely blue eggs of the robin nestled in their cup of mud and twigs.

The young of the American robin have a relatively short incubation period and hatch naked and blind, a state known as altricial; in some species, the eyes are still shut. Totally dependent upon their parents for nourishment, protection and warmth, they complete their development outside the egg, in the safety of the nest. The parents of altricial offspring build strong nests, well anchored to a tree, with high walls to prevent the young from falling out.

SPARROWS

Swamp sparrows hatch after an incubation period of 15 days but do not leave the nest until they are almost two weeks old. When the young, unskilled fliers first leap from the safety of the nest, they risk falling straight into the waiting jaws of frogs, fish and turtles in the marsh below.

Small and scrappy, the house sparrow is suited to life in crowded city environments. It is competitive and willing to fight for food and shelter. As a result, it has become a permanent resident all over North America and much of the world.

When possible, the house sparrow robs other species of nesting sites or makes use of openings available in human architecture, such as in the eaves of buildings or behind loose boards, where it simply heaps straw and leaves together in a pile. The sparrow's natural nest is a covered one built in trees and vines, a more elaborate adaptation for the life it lives. A relative of the African weaver finch, the sparrow creates a dome-shaped woven structure using blades of grass, with a side opening that leads to the nest chamber. The covered nest is water-resistant and windproof and provides good protection for the two or three broods the sparrow raises in a season. Unlike many species, the sparrow overwinters in the north. It remains active all winter and so uses its nest as a sleeping chamber and as a place to raise its hatchlings. The female alone incubates the eggs, but the young are fed insects by both parents.

As annoying as the species can be, it is also highly entertaining and social. One autumn, I saw an unusual sight in the city. On a quiet Sunday

morning, a flicker hammered away on various knots in a tree trunk in a neighbourhood populated by sparrows. A group of six house sparrows appeared and alternately took vocal and physical swipes at the intruder. They chased the flicker around the tree for a few minutes, persistently driving it from one knot to another. In their typical bullying fashion, they were defending their territory. Yet when the flicker finally abandoned its project, the sparrows seemed to lose interest in the tree trunk.

The house sparrow was introduced to this continent in the 19th century by settlers who missed the tiny bird. Although the first attempt to transport sparrows to North American cities failed, the second introduction was a great success — maybe too successful. The population explosion of the house sparrow has taken its toll on other species. Like a human, the house sparrow can survive in disturbed environments; it also shares the human tendency to displace native species from their territories.

The swamp sparrow, a member of the finch family, builds its well-hidden, elevated nest in stands of cattails in the freshwater swamps of Canada and the northern United States. The open cup-style nest is woven from large blades of dry, heavy marsh grasses and lined with finer grasses. Unlike the house sparrow of the weaverbird family, the swamp sparrow is a migratory species that returns annually, in the early spring, to its northern nesting grounds.

The nesting cavity of the flicker is coveted by other birds, and the flicker will fight to defend it. If a flicker abandons its nesting hole, the cavity is immediately inhabited by species such as starlings or bufflehead ducks. Arriving first in the nesting territory, the male flicker drums on trees, fenceposts, electrical poles and even roofs to attract a mate. If he is successful in finding a partner, the male and female work together to construct a nest in the trunk or stump of a dead or decaying tree. Each year, the pair returns to the same site to create a new nesting chamber that they line with fresh wood chips. One flicker was observed excavating in the trunk of a tree already riddled with 34 nesting cavities. The female lays 5 to 10 eggs that are incubated by both parents. After the eggs hatch, the nestlings are fed insects by the adults. They leave the nest after three weeks of parental care. Although the flicker feeds primarily on insects, it locates them in a variety of places other than drilled holes—on the surface of trees, on the ground and in the air. The balance of the flicker's diet is made up of berries and seeds, and it is one of the few species that can survive the toxic effects of poison-ivy berries.

WOODPECKERS

The woodpecker has the disposition of a dedicated artisan: single-minded and hardworking. Chiselling wood is its way of life; it finds its food and creates its nest site by chipping away at trees. With successive strokes of its bill, the bird shatters the decaying bark and then stops, as if listening to the resonance of the wood to determine its quality. In fact, the woodpecker is trying to locate insects beneath the bark.

Its body is a flesh-and-blood woodworking tool. Although narrow, its neck is muscular enough to give its heavy bill the power to endure long hours of pecking. The numbing effect of a life spent pounding trees is eased by the woodpecker's thick skull and by a brain that is insulated with a shock-absorbing cushion of air. Its nostrils are covered with bristles that act like a mask to filter out wood chips and dust—an occupational hazard.

The woodpecker's bill is its chisel. Sharp and strong, it is an effective tool for drilling trees. The woodpecker spends much of its active time hunting for food. When the downy woodpecker drills into a tree and detects insects, it proceeds to chip the bark cover away and lift them out with its specialized tongue, which is barb-tipped and coated with saliva, allowing the woodpecker to reach deep into the holes after the insect larvae.

Downy woodpeckers mate for life and share all the responsibilities of nest building and caring for the young—even the incubation of the eggs. Woodpeckers are called hole-breeders. To hollow out a shelter, the woodpeckers take turns excavating a cavity in a tree. Secure inside the cavity, the woodpecker nest is a fortress, keeping the birds well protected and close to their food source. The cavity is lined with a few leftover wood chips. During mating season, the nest is used to raise the young, but since most woodpeckers overwinter in the north, it becomes a permanent residence.

With few exceptions, woodpecker species have four-toed feet, with two toes facing forward and two toes facing back. The clamplike claws provide a firm anchor, and the stiff, pointed tail is used for support. Both features allow the bird to shuffle up and down the tree to work comfortably from any position.

The woodpecker uses its physical tools in innovative ways. When faced with a tough nut, it resorts to the "woodpecker's anvil." In order to open the nut, the woodpecker picks it up and wedges it firmly in the bark. Once the nut is tightly in place, the bird draws back its head and strikes the nut with its beak until the shell cracks open. If you place a bird feeder in your yard in the winter, when food is in short supply, you might have the opportunity to watch a woodpecker in action.

The pileated woodpecker is the largest woodpecker in Canada. It can reach 20 inches in length and have a wingspan of up to 30 inches. Insects form the bulk of the pileated's diet, so it tends to work around dead and dying trees. To extract wood-boring beetles and to raid the galleries of carpenter ants, the pileated woodpecker excavates holes six inches across and six inches deep. For its nesting site, it prefers tall, dead trees. A pileated pair may return to the same nesting site each year and, together, drill a fresh cavity and line it with leftover wood shavings.

CLIFF SWALLOWS

The barn swallow collects mud and straw to build its nest. The mud bonds the nest to a vertical surface; the straw holds the mud pellets together and adds strength. The male and female work on the construction of the nest for up to two weeks. Barn swallows ordinarily nest as individual pairs, but in a prime nesting site—elevated for open-air foraging flights and close to both water and a source of mud—they build in colonies. A location such as the inside of a building, the eave of a roof or the underside of a bridge protects the water-soluble building material from disintegrating, which is always a risk if the nest is placed in an open area.

The barn swallow nest is an open balcony formed from mud and straw and lined with feathers and animal hair. The female lays up to five eggs, which are incubated by both the male and the female. At about three weeks of age, the young are able to fly but may remain in the family nest for another few weeks. Sometimes, to encourage the young to leave the nest, the adults approach with insects in their beaks and then fly backward, just out of reach. Other parents simply stop feeding the nestlings to force them to leave. Eventually, the birds become such skilful fliers that they can skim over the surface of ponds and streams to drink without landing.

Around mud puddles, riverbanks and tidal flats, flocks of swallows are often seen energetically flapping their wings as they hover inches above the ground. They do their best not to let their wiry little feet touch the cold, wet mud. Chattering loudly and constantly, they occasionally dip into the shore, scooping up beakfuls of mud that they carry away.

The cliff swallow's natural choice for a nesting site is an elevated open area out of the reach of predators. Historically, the swallow has lived on rock cliffs and escarpments. However, the construction of tall buildings, in an accidental imitation of the swallow's chosen habitat, has brought the bird out of its normal environment and closer to the city. The species has grown in population by inhabiting the eaves of towers, bridges and barns. The design of the swallow's nest has made the transition from the wilderness to the city an easy one.

The nest is made exclusively of mud. Unlike the moulded construction of the robin, the cliff swallow's nest is dimply, plastered and built bit by bit from tiny mud pellets that the swallow collects and then shapes in its mouth. Mud is easy to find, and most importantly, it is flexible for building. It sticks to a flat surface and, when dry, is moisture-resistant. Different locations and

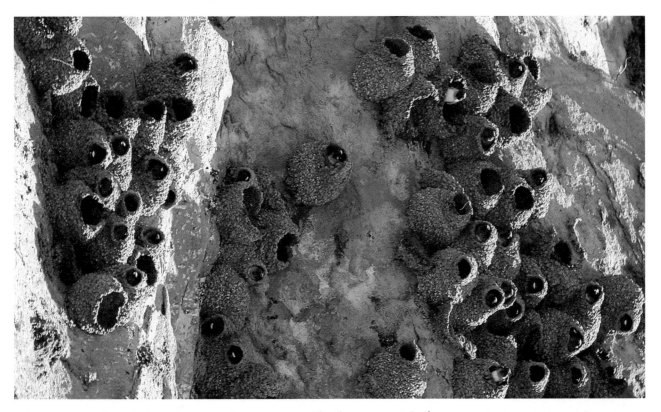

climates require different consistencies of mud.

Pasted to a vertical surface, the swallow's nest is shaped like a half-circle and has a small, protective chutelike opening. It is completely enclosed and draftproof – a good feature for elevated open areas – and lined with grass and feathers.

The cliff swallow requires as many as 1,000 mud pellets to construct its home. When studying cliff swallow nests in colonies of up to 100, you can see the degree of experience of the birds building them.

Some are perfectly symmetrical domes – the pellets of clay are all the same size. Others are lopsided, probably the handiwork of less experienced builders.

Swooping, gliding and banking their way through the sky, swallows scoop up midges, flying ants and other swarming insects. Because they depend on such insects for food, swallows are the earliest fall migrants, leaving when insect populations begin to decline. Many return to the colony and construct the same dense cluster of nests.

Grouped in inaccessible colonies of up to 100, cliff swallow nests are easy to defend. The narrow down-turned neck of the entrance tunnel protects the eggs and the young tucked snugly deep inside. In the event of an attack from a nest-robbing species such as a crow, the entire colony protects the nests by cooperatively mobbing the predator.

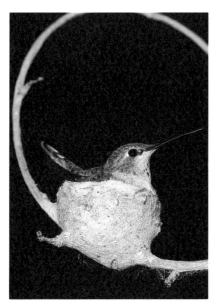

HUMMINGBIRDS

Flying up and down, forward and backward, making sudden starts and stops, the ruby-throated hummingbird whirls around like a tiny helicopter. Its rigid wings are operated by powerful muscles and beat 3,000 to 4,000 times per minute; the little bird moves so fast and with such precision that it appears frozen in midair.

The greatest challenge facing the world's tiniest bird is to maintain a constant body temperature. With a heart that pumps 1,000 times per minute, the hummingbird has a high metabolism and must feed constantly in order to survive. Its long brush-tipped tongue, like that of the bumblebee, is specially adapted for feeding. Deeply cleft, it can be rolled into a tube to suck nectar from the inside of a flower as the bird momentarily hovers and then moves on. The hummingbird copes with extremely cold weather by falling into a sort of nightly torpor; by dropping its metabolic rate, the bird enters a mini hibernation.

To help conserve its body heat, the hummingbird constructs a delicately woven and well-insulated nest. Located in the fork of a tree, the open cup-shaped structure is composed of mosses, dried weed stems and bits of seeds and leaves intertwined with a frame of spider silk. The hummingbird plucks spiders from their webs, then gath-

The Anna's hummingbird is one of more than 300 species of hummingbird, ranging in size from the two-inch Cuban hummingbird, no bigger than a large bumblebee, to the giant tropical hummingbird, which measures 8½ inches in length. The hummingbird's large chest muscles enable it to hover, and its needlelike beak allows it to manipulate spider silk into the frame of its nest, to snatch insects out of the air and to reach deep inside flowers to collect nectar. Hummingbirds and bees share the responsibility of pollinating floral species. Bees are colour-blind to red flowers, while hummingbirds are attracted to that colour. Therefore, hummingbirds pollinate many of the species that bees do not.

Year after year, the female calliope hummingbird returns to her favourite nesting site. The calliope hummingbird prefers sheltered places on the limbs of pine trees or in clusters of cones growing on branches. Using the remains of the previous year's nest as the foundation, she builds a deep 1½-inch-wide cup from grey and brown plant material and chips of bark. The nest is constructed around a network of spider silk and is covered with lichens. The interior is well lined with soft, white cattail, dandelion or milkweed down. It is just wide enough for the female and her two eggs. Unlike other hummingbirds that fall into a nightly torpor, the female of this smaller species can survive near-freezing temperatures in the warmth of the nest.

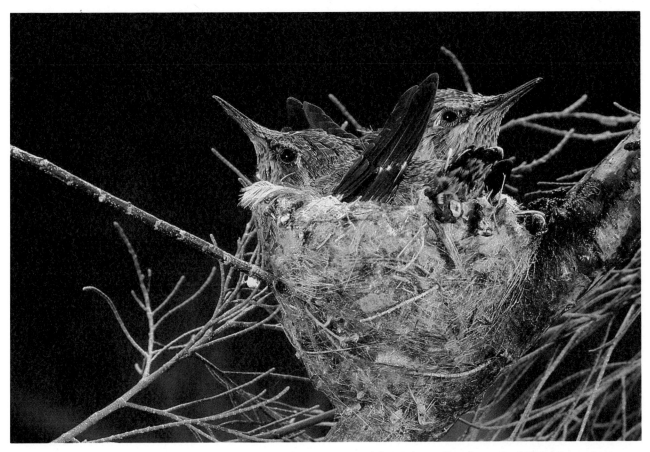

ers the silk and weaves it into the nest. Because spider silk is incredibly tough, it adds flexibility and strength. The hummingbird's unique flying ability allows it to manipulate the silk in a way that no other bird can, finely tucking all of the ends into its little down-filled incubator. Such neatness is accomplished through the use of its delicate and dexterous bill.

The female hummingbird builds the nest on her own, moulding it by sitting inside and twisting her little body back and forth. Sometimes, the construction takes up to three weeks. Situated 5 to 20 feet off the ground, the tiny nest is deep, thick-walled and about two inches in diameter. The interior is amply lined with feathers; the exterior is decorated with lichens, which make the structure look like a natural part of the environment.

On a base of soft plant down, the female Anna's hummingbird lays her eggs before the walls of the nest are erected. Once inside the insulated walls, the female can conserve body heat so that she does not need to go into a state of torpor during incubation. The eggs hatch in a little over two weeks, and the juvenile Anna's hummingbirds can fly three weeks later.

The chimney swift is more comfortable in flight than when it is at rest. Using its sharp claws, it clings awkwardly to a vertical surface; if the swift lands on the ground, it has trouble taking off. Many swifts spend the night on the wing, and some are thought to remain in continuous flight until they reach maturity and construct their first nests, which could be as much as two years and 300,000 miles later. The European swift flies more than 500 miles each day; one banded American chimney swift was estimated to have flown over a million miles during its lifetime. Swifts have been clocked at speeds in excess of 200 miles per hour.

SWIFTS

A swift in flight pumps its wings vigorously in a burst of rapid strokes; then it releases the built-up energy by sailing through sharp dips and dives. The small-bodied bird is an accomplished flier that gets its power from elongated wings, logging more daytime flying hours than any other bird.

The swift is out of place on the ground. Translated from Greek, the swift's family name, Apodidae, means "without feet." In fact, the swift does have feet, but they are weak, tiny and barely visible through its feathers. Clearly not designed for life as a pedestrian, the swift can scarcely stand.

However, the swift never needs to touch the ground – it feeds, drinks and even mates on the wing. When at rest, it is able to cling to a branch or a jagged vertical surface with its strong claws, using its sturdy tail feathers for support.

Like the swallow, the swift forages by flying through the air with its beak open, scooping up hundreds of insects, beetles, ants and spiders. Its range is restricted to areas where such insects are plentiful. During cold spells, adult and hatchling swifts wait out an insect shortage by becoming less active and falling into a temporary torpor.

Although the swift migrates with insect populations, many return each year to a preferred site, often nesting near one another. Their dependence on insects for food makes living together a good choice. Individuals can learn where food sources are by watching the comings and goings of other birds.

The swift selects a protected and dark place such as a chimney, an old abandoned well, a tower or the hollow of an isolated tree.

Most species build a bracket-style nest: an open semicircle attached to a flat, vertical surface. The nest is composed of bits of bark and twigs, which the swift can obtain without landing on the ground. Some nesting materials come from plant matter that the bird snatches out of the air during its routine flights.

The swift has developed a salivary glue that hardens when dry, binding the nesting materials together. It applies the glue by repeatedly flying back and forth from the nest and pulling strings of adhesive. During the breeding season, just prior to the nest-building period, the swift's salivary glands swell to many times their normal size. One Asian swift species constructs its nest solely from the sticky glue – the chief ingredient of bird's-nest soup.

The chimney swift got its name from its frequent choice of nesting site. Unfortunately, it does not recognize the dangers of chimneys and seeks them out because they are warm. If you want to do this world-class flyer a favour, place a screen over the top of your chimney to keep it out.

The chimney swift constructs its nest from twigs and bits of bark that it sometimes breaks off trees with its feet while in flight. To cement the building materials in place, the swift uses a salivary glue that becomes hard when it dries. The eggs of the chimney swift hatch after a three-week incubation that is shared by the male and female. Even as a hatchling, the chimney swift has large wings and the deep, wide beak that will be important later for nest building. The young can fly when they are 30 days old but spend the nights of the next few weeks in the nest.

49

The bald eagle has such specific requirements for its nesting site that fierce battles are often fought to defend existing structures. Bald eagles build huge platform nests at the tops of strong trees. The base is constructed from branches that are roughly piled together until they settle firmly into place. A smaller dish made from grasses and dry vegetation lines the platform and cradles the eggs. The bald eagle can lay up to three eggs, which are incubated by both adults; however, rivalry among the young birds usually results in only one survivor. Eggs hatch in about five weeks, but the immature bird does not grow its adult plumage until it is nearly 4 years old. The bald eagle mates for life and returns annually to the same nesting site, adding new material to the old foundation.

BALD EAGLES

It is always a breathtaking experience to witness a bald eagle in flight. With its full wingspread, the powerful bird soars on gusts of wind and pockets of air that carry it, like a glider, effortlessly over great distances.

Everything about the bald eagle is grand. Impressive specimens, the mature female and male are large birds weighing 8 to 14 pounds; they grow to nearly four feet in length, with wingspans of six to eight feet. Their plumage is dramatic: a hood of white head feathers and a white tail contrast a dark brown body. They have penetrating yellow eyes, large taloned feet and a hooked bill.

The eagle's size and power are appropriately matched by its architectural requirements. The eagle's nest is called a platform and may be 7 to 8 feet across and 12 feet deep. Such a large size limits its location to the tops of tall, strong trees.

Whereas most birds use their beaks to transport building materials, the male and female eagles carry branches up to six feet in length clutched in their talons. The boughs are piled until a suitable base has been created. The nest is lined with moss, pine needles, grass, feathers and leaves. The largest eagle platform ever observed was 10 feet across and 25 feet deep. After a quarter-century of use, all two tons of the accumulated material

crashed to the ground. The choice of nesting site is not just to provide a majestic view; from its elevated eyrie, an eagle — whose vision is almost 10 times as powerful as a human's — can spot a rabbit two miles away and swoop down to seize it in its powerful talons.

Commonly referred to as a bird of prey because it is a carnivore, or meat eater, and targeted for elimination in the past because it was thought to be a threat to other species, the eagle is a spectacular bird of power, grace and daring.

The bald eagle is carnivorous, but its dependence on fish and waterfowl has made it an endangered species. Agricultural pesticides have entered the food chain and have shown up in the diet of the eagle. The side effects include the thinning of the bald eagle's eggshell, which makes the fragile eggs more likely to be damaged during incubation. In many cases, the poisoned adult birds fail to lay fertilized eggs.

They have the best eyesight, hearing and sense of smell in the animal kingdom. Inhabiting land, air and water, in every kind of climate, mammals have the widest assortment of shapes and behaviours of any animals on Earth, ranging in size from the pygmy shrew, no larger than a penny, to the 150-ton blue whale.

With fat and fur to protect them from the cold, mammals can maintain a constant body temperature, which means that many mammals do little or no building. Deer can withstand bad weather by seeking temporary shelter in a cave or a grove of trees. Some mammals, like carnivores, are fierce hunters that can stalk and trap their own food. Large mammals are fast and strong, able to fight or outrun predators.

But smaller mammals, like rodents and insectivores, must build structures to provide shelter, nesting and food-storage areas and protection. They spend a great deal of time and energy fixing and adding onto their homes. Hunted by larger meat eaters, small mammals cannot travel long distances, and so they live within a limited, carefully guarded territory. In winter, cold weather and the lack of vegetation force many mammals into hibernation. For these reasons, most builders occupy permanent structures.

Mammalian builders have sharp claws and teeth that they use to dig and scrape with. Their well-developed forepaws grip sticks and branches, and they are able to lift, carry and manipulate these materials into place.

From the landscape engineering of the beaver to the tree-planting projects of the squirrel to the soil aeration and mixing of the ground-burrowing animals, the architecture of mammals, unlike that of other animals, dramatically shapes the world around us.

Previous page: Its large tail, short limbs and stocky frame make the beaver especially vulnerable when travelling on land. It is much safer for the beaver to transport food and building materials through the water. The deer mouse, above, stays within a limited home territory and often builds its well-insulated nest in the protection of a hollow log. In cold weather, mice huddle together in their nests to conserve heat. A familiar inhabitant of a wide variety of areas, including mature deciduous forests, grassy meadows and brushland, the deer mouse eats seeds, nuts, berries and sometimes insects. In preparation for winter, it stores up to a gallon of seeds in its cache.

By the time these 12-day-old deer mice are weaned at approximately one month of age, the female, probably pregnant with her next litter, will be ready to build a new nest. Although the male is chased away by the female just before she gives birth, he returns in a few weeks to help care for the babies and maintain the nest. The male also takes the young mice on their first foraging expeditions.

MICE

Being small and warm-blooded in a cold world can make life difficult. An animal as tiny as a mouse has little physical bulk in which to store its body heat, so when a mouse is out in the cold, it, too, becomes cold – unless it can find a way to create and retain that heat.

Mice are able to generate a lot of heat for themselves. The smaller the animal, the higher its production of energy, which is determined by the amount of food the animal eats and the amount of activity it performs. Mice have ferocious appetites and speedy hearts that beat almost 500 times per minute. Therefore, their primary problem is not one of heat production but of heat conservation. They have adapted their building skills to save the heat energy they work so hard to produce. As a result, mice have become insulation specialists.

Their nests are constructed of many different kinds of material, depending on the area in which the small rodents live and what they can find there. Some build nests of grass and leaves padded with cattail down, which are warm, soft and cozy. Others, like house mice, use wool, thread, string or even household insulation to weave a fluffy nest. They are all, however, first-rate weavers able to build tight nests designed to keep the heat in and the cold out.

Mice weave balls of grass and then hollow out a tiny interior chamber the size of a ping-pong ball, where they care for their young. Since most mice live less than a year in the wild, the survival of the species depends on its ability to give birth frequently and abundantly; some have up to 14 litters a year, with one to nine offspring per litter. Their nests are built primarily to protect their young from predators and harsh weather conditions.

One of the most delicate mouse nests is woven by the female western harvest mouse. Mainly a plant eater, the harvest mouse builds its nest off the ground in stands of the plants where it lives. Well camouflaged, the nests are basically round balls of grass measuring about three inches across.

The tiny species has grooved front teeth that it uses as a tool for building, a feature which makes it distinct from other species. The mouse climbs the stalk of a plant and makes an A-frame for the nest by bending two stalks toward one another. Using its clawed forepaws to pull the stems of nearby vegetation through its grooved teeth, the harvest mouse shreds the material, which is then woven into the frame of the nest. The walls are built up in much the same way, and the nest is reinforced from the inside. An opening is left on the underside for an entrance. A roof is added, and the interior is lined with shredded leaves and the down of bulrushes.

The female white-footed mouse gives birth to four litters per year, on average, each containing up to nine helpless offspring that require the protective warmth of an insulated nest. They mature in as little as four weeks, but few live past their first year in the wild. Larger and more active than the deer mouse, this tree-climbing species lives primarily in deciduous or shrubby habitats and eats seeds, grasses, nuts and insect larvae.

MOLES

When you look into the face of a star-nosed mole, you cannot help being surprised. It can make your skin crawl. Twenty-two wriggling, rose-coloured tentacles hang from its nose. Maybe you are not seeing clearly—or maybe it is one of nature's eerie mistakes.

It is difficult to imagine the purpose of something so strange. One answer is found in the mole's feeding habits. It uses the touch-sensitive snout to probe and identify its prey—worms, snails, beetle larvae and other insects—in the underground maze of tunnels it creates and inhabits.

Moles dig two types of tunnel. The permanent-residence tunnel may go as deep as three yards and houses the nesting room, food cache and sleeping chamber. The sleeping and nesting areas are widened sections found along the tunnel passageways. Lined with grass and leaves, the tunnels are so deep in the ground that they are warm and secure from predators.

The second type of tunnel is a surface tunnel that the mole uses to travel from one place to another. Surface tunnels are not excavated. Instead, the mole positions its body at a 45-degree angle and ploughs its way along by pushing up loosened dirt.

After the tunnels are completed, the mole sets out on regular patrols

Surface tunnels are used as runways, a means of travelling quickly through its territory. The path of the tunnel follows the texture of the soil and reflects where the earth was the easiest to move. At one time, biologists believed that moles cleared tunnels as they foraged for food. But surface tunnels are actually the mole's method of trapping insects and worms. Much of its time is spent patrolling the excavated tunnels in search of food, while the deeper tunnels it creates are used for nesting and overwintering.

to gather up the worms and bugs that fall into them. In an open field, especially during the spring thaw, you can follow the zigzagging raised tracks of dirt that identify the territory of the solitary, industrious mammal.

Because of its small size, the mole faces the same kinds of problems that confront the mouse, but it has handled them differently. While the mouse constructs an insulated nest that keeps it warm, the mole builds tunnels beneath the frost line that allow it to remain active, well fed and beyond the range of predators.

The mole is ill-suited for travel outside the maze because of the adaptations it has made to spend its life underground. Its eyes and ears are poorly developed; most moles are blind or nearly blind. In the dark underground, normal eyes would be of little use, but when the mole leaves its tunnel and moves above ground, the small mammal becomes easy prey. It cannot see where it is going or what is coming after it and can be attacked by hawks, snakes, owls and even bullfrogs.

With its forelegs positioned on the sides of its compact body and connected directly to its strong shoulders, the mole has evolved as a living shovel. Its paws are large and turned outward, with flat, scaly, reptilian-looking claws. Like a miniature Olympic breaststroker, the mole propels itself forward by clearing the earth away with sideways strokes.

Its coat is the mole's one truly beautiful characteristic: it is dark, rich and velvety. You cannot rub a mole the wrong way. Each hair is hinged so that it can be brushed in any direction and will always feel smooth. Whether moving forward or backward, the mole can travel through tunnels and not ruffle its fur.

Without sufficient nourishment, a mole will die within hours. Because it has to eat most of the time, it collects food whenever it has the opportunity. Researchers have unearthed hundreds of grubs, earthworms and other mole fare squirming in a mole's food cache.

None of us is likely to see a more bizarre-looking creature than the star-nosed mole. Its 22 wriggling tentacles emerge grotesquely from its face as it forages for worms, mollusks and crustaceans along the muddy shores of ponds and streams. The tentacles, known as Eimer's organs, expand and help the mole to locate and identify its prey as it uses its oversize paddlelike claws to burrow through the earth. Its water-repellent fur and wide tail have allowed this mammal to live semi-aquatically; it can dive in water to depths of three feet in search of food and can stay submerged for up to three minutes.

Although some groundhog offspring spend the first winter with their mother in hibernation because they are not strong enough to survive on their own, they usually leave the den as soon as they can take care of themselves. Unlike other members of the squirrel family that can store nuts, the groundhog runs out of food when winter comes. For the months preceding hibernation, it concentrates on building up body fat. During hibernation, an adult groundhog may burn up to one-third of its body weight, and a first-year groundhog may lose up to one-half, even though they use only a fraction of the energy that would be required if they were to remain active during the winter.

GROUNDHOGS

The slow, sleepy groundhog is one of the largest members of the squirrel family, but it has none of the speed or grace of the tree squirrel. And while many ground squirrels are social animals, famous for their affectionate and playful interaction, the groundhog is solitary by nature.

On a walk through a field, you can easily recognize a groundhog burrow by the large mound of dirt at the entrance. Unfortunately, the mound also makes it easy for predators to find the groundhog. And there are many; foxes, wolves, coyotes and bears are all too willing to make a meal of this squirrel. Always aware of the possibility of attack, the groundhog digs numerous exits to its summer foraging den, which is a network of tunnels close to its food source. A tunnel can be as deep as 15 feet and as long as 60 feet. To avoid the risk of flooding, the groundhog carefully builds the tiny internal, or bedroom, chamber on an upward slope.

For further protection against predators, the groundhog digs a series of 1½-foot-deep plunge holes throughout its territory for emergency escapes. When pursued, the groundhog gets away from its attacker by heading for the nearest plunge hole and diving in, falling straight to the bottom. Just deeper than the reach of the predator, the holes provide sufficient room for the groundhog to turn around and climb out when the coast is clear.

The groundhog is a grazer and likes grassy fields rather than forests; its powerful jaws can cut large quantities of vegetation. Happiest in the sunshine, it leaves its burrow only in the daytime, usually early in the morning. It is not uncommon to see one stretched out on a fence rail or rolling around in the dirt in front of its burrow, soaking up the sun. Its short legs make speedy getaways almost impossible, so it surveys the surrounding territory from the safety of the main entrance.

The groundhog's dependence on greenery limits its activity to the growing season. Unlike other squirrels that can cache a winter food supply, the groundhog runs out of vegetation when winter comes. For the months preceding hibernation, then, its main task is to eat and thereby build up body fat.

Located within the forest, its deep winter burrow offers an escape from starvation and freezing temperatures. When it is time to hibernate, the groundhog lines the interior of its sleeping chamber with straw and hay to make a warm, comfortable bed and barricades the opening with as much straw as it can stuff into the tunnel. The fattened groundhog spends the entire winter curled up in a tight ball with its head tucked on its chest to keep warm. It spends four to five months sleeping in its chamber beneath the frost line. The animal's bodily pro-

cesses drop to a fraction of their active rate, and the groundhog breathes only once every six minutes. Over the winter, it may lose up to one-third of its body weight. In fact, hibernation is so demanding that many young groundhogs do not survive it.

The groundhog's solitary life is interrupted during the spring mating season. In March or early April, the female allows other groundhogs in her territory. She produces one litter per season. The male stays in the den until the young are born. Weaned after six weeks, the babies begin to venture above ground and nibble on vegetation. When they can fend for themselves, the young groundhogs are driven out by the mother. In late summer, they wander off to find their own territories and to take up the isolated life of adult groundhogs.

From the opening of its tunnel, a groundhog surveys the surrounding territory for predators, such as hawks, bobcats, coyotes and foxes. Although a groundhog burrow may be up to 60 feet long and feature several emergency exits, there is just one main entrance. While the groundhog's solid frame makes it well adapted for digging, it also leaves the animal vulnerable to attack from its more agile enemies.

An eastern chipmunk, its cheek pouches stuffed with food, peers out of the nest it has built in a tree cavity. A member of the squirrel family, it spends most of its active time collecting roots, seeds and nuts, which it distributes in various caches throughout its territory. Dark stripes down its back and tawny stripes across its cheeks provide the chipmunk with excellent camouflage in the shadows of the daytime forest.

TREE SQUIRRELS

All of us have seen the gymnastic feats of both grey and red tree squirrels. Sharp-clawed forepaws, compact bodies and bushy tails allow these squirrels to race through the treetops, leaping across gaps from branch to branch. Spending most of their lives in trees has developed agility, leaping ability and coordination in the small mammals.

But although we have marvelled at the squirrels' swift and seemingly death-defying acrobatics and can see squirrels every day of the year in any city park, most of us are not so familiar with squirrels' nests, or drays. Built in the crowns of trees, grey and red squirrel nests are usually obscured by the full leaves of summer.

Using their forepaws, squirrels create a frame for the nest by wedging several support branches against a fork in the tree. Then they insert smaller leafy branches, moving them around until they are solidly in place. Leaves and other plant material are used to fill the gaps between the branches and to disguise the exterior so that the nest will blend in with the surroundings. The walls are built up to make it spherical, with a side opening for the entrance. The inside is lined with leaves, grass and bark. Squirrels often construct additional nests throughout their territories, which they use as resting spots rather than as homes for their offspring.

Tree squirrels may also build their nests inside the hollow trunk or branch of a mature or rotten tree. They make the same type of lining from leaves and bark as they would for a leaf nest. Sometimes, the cavity nest is used as a winter residence or for raising young, since it is more stable and better protected from the elements than the leafy dray.

During the mating season the male and female share the main nest. But when the female is about to give birth, she chases the male away and becomes completely responsible for the rearing of her two to four helpless, naked and blind offspring. She feeds, cleans, protects and moves them if necessary. When the young are able to leave the nest, she guides them out to climb on the branches of their home tree.

Since they do not hibernate in winter, tree squirrels are great hoarders, gathering and storing food while supplies are plentiful. Grey squirrels prefer the seeds of maple, oak and hickory trees, which they cache in holes in the ground throughout their territories. In spite of the grey squirrel's keen sense of smell, many of the buried seeds are forgotten and eventually grow into trees. Red squirrels prefer to harvest and collect large quantities of pine cones, which they store in piles up to three feet deep.

The survival of tree squirrels in our cities has perhaps been aided by the fact that their natural enemies,

such as the weasel, mink, red fox, raccoon, skunk, bobcat and owl, have all been driven from urban areas. One of the city squirrel's biggest enemies now is the automobile. Another is mange mites, which it picks up as a result of constantly reusing old nest sites.

It is easy to take these energetic mammals for granted. But because they rely on trees for their livelihood, their ongoing presence depends on our ability to maintain a healthy supply of wooded areas in our cities.

A red squirrel cache can measure up to three feet deep and several yards across. Although it has more meat in its diet than other arboreal species do, the red squirrel harvests heavy crops of conifer cones for the winter by stripping all the cones from a tree and then gathering them up. To preserve the cones and to ensure that they will not lose their nutritious seeds, the squirrel chooses shady, humid storage sites. The long-term planning efforts of the red squirrel are often thwarted when its caches are raided by foresters who use the fresh seeds for planting.

POCKET GOPHERS

The pocket gopher, a little bulldozer that weighs less than half a pound, churns up more than a ton of soil each year digging underground tunnels in search of food. Equipped with long, curved claws, and eyelids and ear valves that seal tightly to keep out dust particles, the pocket gopher eats plant tubers, stems and roots. It gets its name from the fur-lined mouth pouch that can be turned inside out to remove the bits of grit and grime which gather there when it eats underground vegetation.

Using its claws and incisors to loosen the soil, the pocket gopher digs with its powerful forelegs in alternating strokes, piling the earth beneath its body. It uses its hind feet to kick the dirt to one side, then turns around and, with forelimbs outstretched, thrusts itself with all its strength off its hind legs, ploughing the loosened soil upward. This method of excavation leaves a distinctive fan-shaped soil pattern at the surface, a telltale sign that a gopher is in the vicinity.

Each species of pocket gopher has a different body size, which may be largely determined by geography and soil conditions. Although larger and stronger species inhabit harder soil, all pocket gophers avoid rocky terrain that is impossible to excavate. The smaller northern pocket gopher found in Canada lives in a

The path of the pocket gopher burrow varies according to the presence of the roots and tubers that make up the gopher's food source. Since each individual animal is capable of moving one ton of soil in a year, a colony of gophers can wreak havoc on a farmer's field. Superbly adapted to a life of underground foraging, the pocket gopher has a short tail, small eyes and tiny ears and can orient itself in the dark by the use of hairs on its tail and its loose-fitting skin, both of which are sensitive to changes in movement, tension and pressure. Its burrows bring many benefits to plants and wildlife. In addition to aerating the soil and mixing it, by bringing new mineral-rich earth to the surface, the pocket gopher creates burrows that provide shelter for species such as salamanders, toads, lizards, skunks, turtles, weasels, rabbits and even burrowing owls.

variety of soil types but seems to prefer moist, soft soil. Although it can tolerate the low oxygen level of its underground environment, no species can survive dense, overly wet clay.

The burrow method is an energy-intensive form of feeding, providing the gopher with the bulbs and roots that it likes to eat. The pocket gopher's time- and energy-saving strategy is to build a tunnel just wide enough for it to fit through. Like other burrowing animals, the pocket gopher has two kinds of tunnel: a shallow one used for feeding and transport and a deeper one in which it lives. The residence tunnel contains a nesting chamber well beneath the frost line. Unable to stand extreme climates, the pocket gopher needs a resting burrow that offers protection from both heat and cold.

When inside the burrow, the gopher blocks the entrance with soil to prevent flooding and to protect itself and its offspring from predators. Most pocket gopher predators, such as the weasel, skunk, fox and badger, cannot afford to use the energy required to dig a gopher out of its burrow. Since the protected environment of the burrow ensures a high survival rate for the offspring, the pocket gopher gives birth to small litters.

The mating ritual involves an unusual burrowing behaviour. The pocket gopher, like the groundhog, lives alone except during the mat-

ing season. To find a mate, the larger, more powerful male leaves his burrow and begins to tunnel in a straight line until he finds a receptive female. Although it may seem a haphazard approach, it is a sound strategy. Plotting a straight course increases the male's chances of encountering females. After mating, though, both sexes resume their solitary existence.

When the snow melts on the prairies, tunnel tracks emerge – a record of the gopher's winter foraging. For the farmer, the energetic animal is a mixed blessing. While the gopher is credited with blending and aerating the deep grassland soil of the region, it also tends to eat the roots of crop plants and creates a labyrinth of hazards for livestock.

The large, curved claws on both its front and hind feet help the pocket gopher dig underground passageways. The gopher uses its teeth and front claws to loosen the soil during excavation. As with all rodents, its incisors are razor-sharp and never stop growing, but the pocket gopher sets a record. Its teeth grow so quickly that without the wear and tear of constant use in the gritty burrow, they would become longer than the gopher's body in just one year.

MUSKRATS

The muskrat is a giant member of the same family as the vole. Most voles are the size of a house mouse, but the muskrat's large size enables it to do things a little vole cannot. Thanks to its broad, flat rudder of a tail and its large, clawed and webbed hind feet, it can swim and is in less danger of becoming food for pike, bass or other large fish. It feeds on the rich growth of water weeds and marsh plants.

Because the muskrat inhabits a variety of wet areas, including marshes, streams and open lakes, it has devised clever construction techniques to protect itself from its enemies. The versatile builder designs its structures to fit the surroundings. To take up residence on an elevated riverbank, for instance, it begins digging a nest beneath the surface of the water and burrows upward into the riverbank until it is above the waterline. In an open area, the muskrat uses cattails, bulrushes and other reeds to build a raised lodge. Elevated three to four feet above the water level, the structure is mortared with mud. When the lodge is in need of repairs, the muskrat reinforces it from the outside.

The interior of the muskrat's home contains a sleeping chamber comfortably lined with bedding made of grass and other plant matter. "Drier" is the only way to de-

Actually a large vole that can weigh up to three pounds, the muskrat is well adapted for an aquatic existence. It has big, webbed hind feet that are turned slightly outward and act like flippers, making the muskrat a strong swimmer, and a long, broad, naked tail that functions as a rudder and powers the muskrat underwater. The muskrat's coat consists of a thick, waterproof underfur covered with long, glossy, irregular-looking guard hairs. Despite its dense coat, the muskrat can suffer from heat loss if it remains in the water, yet feeding out of the water is also risky. Once exposed, the muskrat is an easy target for attack by horned owls, marsh hawks and ravens.

scribe the interior of the cavity; since all the nesting material is brought through the underwater entrance, it is never completely dry.

The underwater entrance is an important safeguard against intruders, and the muskrat is careful to maintain it. As the water level fluctuates, the muskrat must make sure that the entrance remains concealed beneath the surface, extending the tunnel as required. The mink, a fierce member of the weasel family, can swim and dive and is the one predator capable of trapping the muskrat in its home. As a precaution against such an attack, the muskrat builds its home with more than one entrance.

There are two other typical muskrat constructions: the feeding platform and the push-up. Since its feet and tail are hairless, the muskrat loses a lot of heat in its pursuit of food. To counteract the problem, the muskrat creates a feeding platform by heaping together a quantity of reeds and plants in the form of a raft. By using the raft to lift itself out of the water during feeding, it does not have to eat standing in cold water or on shore, which is even more dangerous.

The push-up, or breathing hole, is a seasonal structure. Although the muskrat lives in lakes and streams deep enough not to freeze solid during the winter months, the icy surface restricts the supply of food. Wherever it finds a hole in the ice, the muskrat piles vegetation

over it. The vegetation keeps the hole free of ice, and the muskrat can use it as an escape route. It also provides a sheltered place for the muskrat to feed. Unfortunately, as the only green vegetation visible in the winter, the push-ups are often disturbed by hungry deer. When that happens, the insulating material covering the hole is lost, and it freezes over.

The muskrat lives the life of a fugitive. Being a favourite food of many larger creatures has forced it to develop sound architectural tactics that allow the muskrat to thrive on the vegetation in our lakes, ponds and rivers.

Cattails are one of the muskrat's most important sources of food and building materials, and its regular harvest of cattails keeps the water in marshes open and attractive to waterfowl all over North America. Visible in every roadside ditch and swamp where there are bulrushes and cattails, muskrat lodges are constructed in the autumn to last through the winter. The lodge is one of the structures the muskrat builds to protect itself from its many enemies on land, in the air and in the water. In the summer, the muskrat abandons it, thus creating welcome housing for waterfowl, which often use the lodge as a nesting site.

Situated in the safety of the beaver pond upstream from the dam, the beaver lodge is constructed from the leftovers of the trees the beavers cut for food. The roof of the lodge is woven in a dome shape from branches and twigs. In the winter, beavers in northern climates use mud to seal the roof and make it waterproof. Young trees with small branches are the favourite choice of building material for the beaver, not only because they tend to be juicier and make better food but also because they are less awkward to transport. Despite the abundance of growth on larger trees, the beaver cuts these only when they are situated close to the water. The amount of time required to fell and transport a large tree, even with help, keeps the beaver on land and at risk of attack.

BEAVERS

From the shore of a tree-lined river or stream at dusk, you might see the arrow-shaped wake of a beaver as it swims silently from its lodge. When it reaches land and hauls its sturdy frame onto the bank, it is heading out to do what it does best. Minutes later, you may hear rustling leaves as the beaver fells the thin and tender aspen trees it loves to eat.

Before settlers arrived and began trapping the large, flat-tailed rodent, the Canadian beaver was found in every stream, pond and lake in the country. The original landscape architect, the beaver is able to shape its environment to suit the life it likes to live.

The beaver – a real heavyweight among rodents – weighs up to 90 pounds when fully grown. Built to live a semiaquatic life, it has a sturdy skeleton, muscular legs and large, webbed hind feet like a duck's. Its flat tail acts like a rudder as it moves through the water and props the beaver upright on land. A powerful swimmer, it easily transports branches in its mouth or under its chin. If it has to, the beaver can remain underwater for up to 15 minutes. Like a submarine, the animal prepares itself before diving: its nostrils shut tightly, valves close over its ears, lips seal its mouth, and a membrane protects its eyes.

But the beaver's teeth are its most important tool, enabling it to harvest and eat food unavailable to other rodents. The stout, sharp teeth can chisel through the heavy bark of three-foot-thick tree trunks to expose the sap-lined inner layers that it likes to eat. The beaver uses vegetation to its full advantage – first as food, then as material for construction.

The beaver family is called a colony, and together, its members choose a site and begin to perform their impressive feats of hydro engineering. Beavers are very particular about their habitats and will go to amazing lengths to tailor their surroundings. To occupy an open lake or pond, they construct a dam, which is their method for controlling the depth of the water. When the water is too shallow, the dam serves to slow the flow, making the pond deep enough for the site of the lodge; the water level can also be lowered by opening the dam.

Construction of the dam begins when the beaver piles brush and branches across the stream, using the leftovers from the living trees it eats. Since green wood is very heavy and will not float away, it makes a solid foundation upon which the dam can be built. The beaver has five-toed forepaws that enable it to grip and drag branches to the site and jam them into the bottom of the stream. The holes in the dam are filled with tree limbs, mud and rocks.

After they have cut down all of

All members of the beaver colony share equally in the construction of the lodge and dam, the expansion of the feeding ground and the defence of the territory. The dam itself requires constant maintenance, since the water in the pond must be kept at a certain level for the security of the lodge and its inhabitants. When a break occurs, the beaver responds quickly, bringing branches, mud and rocks to the site for repairs. Beavers are such conscientious caretakers that trappers intentionally open the dams to lure the beavers out of the safety of their lodge to make the necessary repairs.

The beaver is the second largest rodent in North America and is a strong swimmer, capable of towing large branches through the water and into the food-storage compartment inside the lodge. Like the muskrat, the beaver is adapted to an aquatic existence—when diving, it can close valves over its ears and nostrils and has a protective membrane over its eyes—and so can easily swim to the underwater entrance of the lodge. The submerged entryway keeps out most predators; however, there are some, such as otters and mink, that can swim to the entrance and trap the beaver inside.

This young beaver will remain in the lodge with its mother until it is weaned at 4 weeks of age. It is one of up to nine offspring in the single litter produced each year. When it reaches adulthood, the beaver will find a mate and begin a lifelong relationship. It is such partnerships that form the basis of the colonies.

the nearby trees, the beavers must be able to get to the outlying forest area for additional food and building supplies. From the still pond formed by the dam, they dig canals and channels in order to flood surrounding areas, creating access to new food sources as well as an easy way to transport building materials. Hauling logs overland is a difficult task, so like lumberjacks, beavers float branches to the building site.

Upstream, the beavers create an island, piling together water-drenched logs and tree branches for a place to build their lodge. Above the water surface, they weave a dome from stems and branches, leaving an entrance tunnel underwater to keep the lodge safe from predators. Northern beavers waterproof the roof with mud, which hardens and seals out the cold and the melting snow.

The inside of the lodge is divided into a number of rooms: a living chamber, a winter food cache and a bathroom. Since the lodge is the beavers' permanent home, the bathroom is at the water's edge so that the living space is not soiled. During the spring, when the young are born, the female lives in the lodge alone, while the others gather food to feed the newborn. Offspring remain with the colony for a couple of years until overcrowding forces some of them to leave to establish their own territories.

Maintenance and upkeep are

constant pressures for the beaver colony. Checking the water level, inspecting the dam, harvesting food and territory expansion are all part of the everyday routine. Such hard work makes any beaver property valuable real estate, especially for the offspring still living in the lodge, which stand to inherit it when their parents die.

Beaver construction has consequences for human real estate too, as it dictates how our wetlands look and what plants and wildlife survive there. When beavers cut the big trees around their pond, bushes and tender sprouts shoot up from the tree stumps. The small branches and water-loving, fast-growing plants like willow, aspen and poplar are the beavers' favourite food, and like hardworking farmers, they harvest the crops that spring up in the bright sunlight.

The beaver colony builds a dam to control the depth of the water in an open area. By slowing the flow of water, the dam makes the pond deep enough for the site of the colony's lodge. If the lodge is flooded, the beavers can lower the water level by opening the dam, which can bridge a narrow stream or cross a lake hundreds of yards wide.

CREDITS